DEC 2 0 2010

17(5)

D1316727

Listening to God

with Mother Teresa

Listening to God

with Mother Teresa

Compiled by
WOODEENE KOENIG-BRICKER

Our Sunday Visitor Publishing Division
Our Sunday Visitor, Inc.
Huntington, Indiana 46750

CONTENTS

INTRODUCTION

BLESSED MOTHER TERESA OF Calcutta is one of those iconic figures of our time who needs little introduction. Her bent, sari-clad figure has entered our history books, and even those who did not know of her when she was alive cannot help but have heard of her unending work for the poor of the world.

If her legacy showed any signs of waning, the recent revelations of her inner struggles with faith and hope have introduced this little giant of a woman to another generation. Hundreds of books have been written about her, and numerous collections of her words have been compiled. In this small volume, I have attempted to find some of her lesser-known sayings and match them with the Scriptural teachings on which she based her entire life. Sometimes, her words echo the Scriptures directly; other times, they are rooted in her deep, lifelong understanding of Catholic tradition and teaching. In all cases, they are grounded and centered in a profound and passionate love of Jesus, which spills over in an abiding love for all of God's creation, particularly the poor and downtrodden.

As I saturated myself in Mother's words and then sought to find Scripture that reflected her ideas, I was filled with a sense of enormous peace and blessing — one might even say guidance. In a very real way, I became aware that as we open ourselves to the working of the Spirit, be it serving the poor in the streets of Calcutta or attempting to use our ability for research and writing, the Divine Love, which permeates and pervades all of Creation, stands ready and willing to support us in our endeavors.

If there is one lesson I've learned from Mother's thoughts it is that when we listen to the call of God in our lives, we will never be truly alone on our journey. She says, "You have to be holy where you are — wherever God has put you." I would add that wherever God has put you, he is there with you. You have only to ask for his assistance.

May Mother Teresa's words inspire you to be holy — wherever you are right now.

— Woodeene Koenig-Bricker

1. A Cause of Joy

BE A CAUSE OF joy to others.
Speak well of everyone.
Smile at all you meet.
Deliberately make three acts of loving kindness every day.
Confess any sin against charity.
If you offend anyone — even a small child — ask forgiveness before going to bed.

"Do to others as you would have them do to you."

— LUKE 6:31

2. ATTITUDE OF GRATITUDE

THE BEST WAY TO show your gratitude to God and to people is to accept everything with joy.

"We welcome this in every way and everywhere with utmost gratitude."

— ACTS 24:3

3. WONDERFULLY MADE

I AM NOT HERE JUST to fill a place, just to be a number. He has made me for a purpose. He will fulfill it if I don't put any obstacle in his way.

For it was you who formed my inward parts;
*   you knit me together in my mother's womb.*
I praise you, for I am fearfully and wonderfully made.
*   Wonderful are your works;*
that I know very well.

— PSALM 139:13-14

13

4. Solidarity with the Poor

WHEN OUR POOR ARE going through such hard times in regard to food, light, and water, do we give up food that is not absolutely necessary to our health and nutrition? Do we try not to eat outside of regular meals except in times of sickness? Do we take care to use water and light carefully, turning off the taps and putting out any unnecessary lights?

When I heard these words I sat down and wept, and mourned for days, fasting and praying before the God of heaven.

— NEHEMIAH 1:4

5. Live in Today

You must forgive and forget all the difficult things of yesterday for yesterday is gone. Tomorrow has not yet come. But you have today to love Jesus as he loves you, with a deep personal love.

Yet you do not even know what tomorrow will bring. What is your life? For you are a mist that appears for a little while and then vanishes.

— James 4:14

6. CHAINS OF SIN

IF WE ARE HIDING or controlled by sin, we cannot be free. Sin is like a chain. It destroys life. Confession is as important to Jesus as it to us. It is a joint action . . . Jesus and me.

If we confess our sins, he who is faithful and just will forgive us our sins and cleanse us from all unrighteousness.

— 1 JOHN 1:9

7. MOTHER OF GOD

[MARY] HAD BEEN CHOSEN as the Queen of Heaven and Earth, yet she did not go in search of glory or even to tell Joseph. The first thing she did as the Mother of God was to go in haste to serve her cousin Elizabeth.

In those days Mary set out and went with haste to a Judean town in the hill country, where she entered the house of Zechariah and greeted Elizabeth.

— LUKE 1:39-40

8. Spirit of God, Will of the Father

Come, O blessed Spirit of knowledge and light, and grant that I may perceive the will of the Father. Show me the nothingness of earthly things, that I may realize their vanity and use them only for your glory and my own salvation, looking ever beyond them to you and your eternal reward.

Now we have received not the spirit of the world, but the Spirit that is from God, so that we may understand the gifts bestowed on us by God. And we speak of these things in words not taught by human wisdom but taught by the Spirit, interpreting spiritual things to those who are spiritual.

— 1 Corinthians 2:12–13

9. Fruit of Pride

Moodiness is nothing else but the fruit of pride.

Those who are patient stay calm until the right moment, and then cheerfulness comes back to them.

— Ecclesiasticus 1:23

10. Love Transforms Work

I PRAY THAT YOU WILL understand the words of Jesus, "Love one another as I have loved you." Ask yourself, "How has he loved me? Do I really love others in the same way?" Unless this love is among us, we can kill ourselves with work and it will be only work, not love. Work without love is slavery.

"I give you a new commandment, that you love one another. Just as I have loved you, you also should love one another. By this everyone will know that you are my disciples, if you have love for one another."

— JOHN 13:34-35

11. FALSE HUMILITY

HIDING THE GIFTS GOD has given you or doing your work in an inefficient way is not humility.

"You are the light of the world. A city built on a hill cannot be hidden. No one after lighting a lamp puts it under the bushel basket, but on the lampstand, and it gives light to all in the house. In the same way, let your light shine before others, so that they may see your good works and give glory to your Father in heaven."

— MATTHEW 5:14-16

12. OUR NEED FOR FORGIVENESS

RECEIVE FORGIVENESS TO GIVE forgiveness.

Bear with one another, and if anyone has a complaint against another, forgive each other; just as the Lord has forgiven you, so you also must forgive.

— COLOSSIANS 3:13

13. No Secrets

Never stop to do anything secretly. Hiding is the beginning of lying, a lie in action.

> *"For nothing is hidden that will not be disclosed, nor is anything secret that will not become known and come to light."*
>
> — Luke 8:17

14. One Body in Christ

We finish in each other what is wanting to be in Christ.

For just as the body is one and has many members, and all the members of the body, though many, are one body, so it is with Christ.
— 1 Corinthians 12:12

15. God Is God

SOME CALL HIM ISHWAR, some call him Allah, some simply God, but we all have to acknowledge that it is he who made us for greater things.

"Whoever is not against us is for us."

— MARK 9:40

16. WORD BECOME FLESH

CHRIST CAME INTO THE world to put charity in its proper perspective.

And the Word became flesh and lived among us, and we have seen his glory, the glory as of a father's only son, full of grace and truth. . . . From his fullness we have all received, grace upon grace.

— JOHN 1:14, 16

17. "I Thirst"

I THIRST. HEAR YOUR OWN name, not just once — If you listen with your hearts, you will hear, you will understand. Jesus' thirst hidden in the distressing disguise of the poorest of the poor. This thirst is a reality. He thirsts, I quench.

After this, when Jesus knew that all was now finished, he said (in order to fulfill the scripture), "I am thirsty." A jar full of sour wine was standing there. So they put a sponge full of the wine on a branch of hyssop and held it to his mouth.

— JOHN 19:28-29

18. Teach Us How to Pray

Do not have long discussions on prayer. Learn from Jesus how to pray and allow him to pray in and through you. Then put the fruit of that prayer into living action by loving one another as Jesus loves you.

"When you are praying, do not heap up empty phrases as the Gentiles do; for they think that they will be heard because of their many words. Do not be like them, for your Father knows what you need before you ask him."

— Matthew 6:7-8

19. A Chosen People

HE HAS CHOSEN US; we have not first chosen him.

For you are a people holy to the Lord your God; it is you the Lord has chosen out of all the peoples on earth to be his people, his treasured possession.

— DEUTERONOMY 14:2

20. BLESSED BY THE FATHER

HUNGRY FOR LOVE, HE looks at you.
Thirsty for kindness, he begs from you.
Naked for loyalty, he hopes in you.
Sick and imprisoned for friendship, he wants from you.
Homeless for shelter in your heart, he asks of you.
Will you be that one to him?

"Then the king will say to those at his right hand, 'Come, you that are blessed by my Father, inherit the kingdom prepared for you from the foundation of the world; for I was hungry and you gave me food, I was thirsty and you gave me something to drink, I was a stranger and you welcomed me, I was naked and you gave me clothing, I was sick and you took care of me, I was in prison and you visited me.'"

— MATTHEW 25:34-37

21. GIVING JESUS

LIKE MARY, LET US be full of zeal to go in haste to give Jesus to others.

When Elizabeth heard Mary's greeting, the child leapt in her womb. And Elizabeth was filled with the Holy Spirit and exclaimed with a loud cry, "Blessed are you among women, and blessed is the fruit of your womb. And why has this happened to me, that the mother of my Lord comes to me?"

— LUKE 1:41-43

22. Satisfy Our Hunger

Jesus made himself bread, to satisfy our hunger for God.

"I am the living bread that came down from heaven. Whoever eats of this bread will live for ever; and the bread that I will give for the life of the world is my flesh."

— John 6:51

23. Blessed Are the Meek

We must work hard every day to conquer ourselves. We must learn to be meek and humble of heart.

"Blessed are the meek, for they will inherit the earth."

— Matthew 5:5

24. SELF-KNOWLEDGE AND HUMILITY

SELF-KNOWLEDGE PUTS US ON our knees and it is very necessary for love. For knowledge of God produces love, and knowledge of self produces humility.

For the fear of the Lord is wisdom and discipline, fidelity and humility are his delight.

— ECCLESIASTICUS 1:27

25. FIDELITY TO SMALL THINGS

FIDELITY TO SMALL THINGS will lead you to Christ. Infidelity to small things will lead you to sin.

"His master said to him, 'Well done, good and trustworthy slave; you have been trustworthy in a few things, I will put you in charge of many things; enter into the joy of your master.' "

— MATTHEW 25:23

26. GOD'S WILL BE DONE

I ASK HIM TO MAKE a saint of me, yet I must leave to him the choice of the saintliness itself and still more the means which leads to it.

And going a little farther, he threw himself on the ground and prayed, "My Father, if it is possible, let this cup pass from me; yet not what I want but what you want."

—MATTHEW 26:39

27. WORKING TOGETHER

WHAT WE ARE DOING, you cannot do. And what you are doing, we cannot do. But together, we are doing something beautiful for God.

Indeed, the body does not consist of one member but of many . . . God arranged the members in the body, each one of them, as he chose. If all were a single member, where would the body be? As it is, there are many members, yet one body.

— 1 CORINTHIANS 12:14-20

28. NET OF LOVE

JOY IS A NET of love by which we can catch souls. God loves a person who gives joyfully and the person who gives joyfully gives more.

Each of you must give as you have made up your mind, not reluctantly or under compulsion, for God loves a cheerful giver.

— 2 CORINTHIANS 9:7

29. All Things Are Possible

Persuaded of our nothingness and with the blessing of obedience, we attempt all things, doubting nothing, for with God all things are possible.

Jesus looked at them and said, "For mortals it is impossible, but not for God; for God all things are possible."

— Mark 10:27

30. TOMORROW

WE WILL NOT WORRY about tomorrow but will live the present moment intensely, with complete trust in God.

"So do not worry about tomorrow, for tomorrow will bring worries of its own. Today's trouble is enough for today."

— MATTHEW 6:34

31. A Cheerful Heart

CHEERFULNESS IS OFTEN A cloak which hides a life of sacrifice, continual union with God, fervor, and generosity.

Whether rich or poor, his heart is content,
and at all times his face is cheerful.

— ECCLESIASTICUS 26:4

32. The Need for Joy

Joy is not simply a matter of temperament. In the service of God and souls, it is always hard to be joyful — all the more reason why we should try to acquire it and make it grow in our hearts.

You show me the path of life.
In your presence there is fullness of joy;
in your right hand are pleasures for evermore.

— Psalm 16:11

33. FILLED WITH THE SPIRIT

EVEN ALMIGHTY GOD CANNOT fill what is already full. We must be empty if we want God to fill us with his fullness.

Be filled with the Spirit.

— EPHESIANS 5:18

34. Unchanging Lord

Yesterday is always today to God.

Jesus Christ is the same yesterday and today and forever.
— Hebrews 13:8

35. TEMPLE OF THE HOLY SPIRIT

WE WOULD NEVER DREAM of using dirty, torn cloth as a tabernacle veil to cover the door of the dwelling that Christ chose for himself on earth since his Ascension into heaven. In the same way, we should never cover the temple of the Holy Spirit, which is our body, with torn, dirty, untidy clothes.

Do you not know that your body is a temple of the Holy Spirit within you, which you have from God, and that you are not your own?
— I CORINTHIANS 6:19

36. GOD'S GIFT OF HIMSELF

ASK AND SEEK, AND your heart will grow big enough to receive him and keep him as your own.

"So I say to you, Ask, and it will be given to you; search, and you will find; knock, and the door will be opened for you. For everyone who asks receives, and everyone who searches finds, and for everyone who knocks, the door will be opened."

— LUKE 11:9-10

37. Be Strong

Do not wait for leaders; do it alone, person-to-person.

"Take action, for it is your duty, and we are with you; be strong, and do it."

— Ezra 10:4

38. JUDGE NOT

IF YOU JUDGE PEOPLE, you have no time to love them.

"Do not judge, and you will not be judged; do not condemn, and you will not be condemned. Forgive, and you will be forgiven."

— LUKE 6:37

39. ANIMALS OF THE EARTH

I LOVE ST. FRANCIS OF Assisi, because he had a great love for animals. He used to talk with them and play with them — and scold them if they did harm to anybody. I love animals, too. Animals are such simple creations of God's beauty.

And God said, "Let the earth bring forth living creatures of every kind: cattle and creeping things and wild animals of the earth of every kind." And it was so. God made the wild animals of the earth of every kind, and the cattle of every kind, and everything that creeps upon the ground of every kind. And God saw that it was good.

— GENESIS 1:24-25

40. THE REST WILL BE GIVEN

LET US MORE AND more insist on raising funds of love, of kindness, of understanding, of peace. Money will come if we seek first the kingdom of God; the rest will be given.

"But strive first for the kingdom of God and his righteousness, and all these things will be given to you as well."

— MATTHEW 6:33

41. A Burning Heart

IT IS IMPOSSIBLE TO walk rapidly and be unhappy.

"Were not our hearts burning within us while he was talking to us on the road, while he was opening the scriptures to us?"

— LUKE 24:32

42. Not Like Other People

MANY PEOPLE ARE TALKING *about* the poor, but very few people talk *to* the poor.

Live in harmony with one another; do not be haughty, but associate with the lowly; do not claim to be wiser than you are.

— ROMANS 12:16

43. Enduring Testing

I KNOW GOD WILL NOT give me anything I can't handle. I just wish that he didn't trust me so much.

No testing has overtaken you that is not common to everyone. God is faithful, and he will not let you be tested beyond your strength, but with the testing he will also provide the way out so that you may be able to endure it.

— 1 CORINTHIANS 10:13

44. Light a New Light

Go out into the world today and love the people you meet. Let your presence light new light in the hearts of people.

"In the same way, let your light shine before others, so that they may see your good works and give glory to your Father in heaven."

— Matthew 5:16

45. SHARING POVERTY

Do we treat the poor as our dustbins to give whatever we cannot use or eat? I cannot eat this food, so I will give it to the poor. I cannot use this thing or that piece of cloth, so I will give it to the poor. Am I then sharing the poverty of the poor?

Those who despise their neighbors are sinners, but happy are those who are kind to the poor.

— PROVERBS 14:21

46. TO SERVE THE LORD

IT IS POSSIBLE THAT I may not be able to keep my attention fully on God while I work, but God doesn't demand that I do so. Yet I can fully desire and intend that my work be done with Jesus and for Jesus.

Render service with enthusiasm, as to the Lord and not to men and women.

—EPHESIANS 6:7

47. The Honor of Humility

IT TAKES HUMILITY TO recognize the greatness of God shining through us.

My child, honor yourself with humility,
and give yourself the esteem you deserve.

— ECCLESIASTICUS 10:28

48. LOVE OF NEIGHBOR

WE CANNOT SAY, "I love God, but I don't love my neighbor."

Those who say, "I love God", and hate their brothers or sisters, are liars; for those who do not love a brother or sister whom they have seen, cannot love God whom they have not seen.

— I JOHN 4:20

49. FAITHFULNESS OF GOD

GOD WILL NEVER, NEVER, never let us down if we have faith and put our trust in him.

Commit your way to the Lord;
  trust in him, and he will act.

— PSALM 37:5

50. SERVICE, NOT CRITICISM

LET'S FOCUS MORE ON the things we ought to do in serving our husband, our wife, our children, our brothers — rather than on other people's shortcomings.

"You hypocrite, first take the log out of your own eye, and then you will see clearly to take the speck out of your neighbor's eye."

— MATTHEW 7:5

51. TRUE JUSTICE

LOVE, TENDERNESS, AND COMPASSION are real justice. Justice
without love is not justice.

He has told you, O mortal, what is good;
and what does the LORD require of you
but to do justice, and to love kindness,
and to walk humbly with your God?

— MICAH 6:8

52. Giving Alms

WE RECEIVE [MONEY] WITH our right hand and we give it away with our left.

"But when you give alms, do not let your left hand know what your right hand is doing."

— MATTHEW 6:3

53. CHRIST'S STRENGTH

[CHRIST] COMES AND USES us to be his love and compassion in the world in spite of our weakness and frailties.

Therefore I am content with weaknesses, insults, hardships, persecutions, and calamities for the sake of Christ; for whenever I am weak, then I am strong.

— 2 CORINTHIANS 12:10

54. THE POWER OF PRAYER

IF YOU ARE CAPABLE of bringing prayer back into your homes, you will be equally capable of overcoming all of the hardships that afflict the world.

Therefore confess your sins to one another, and pray for one another, so that you may be healed. The prayer of the righteous is powerful and effective.

— JAMES 5:16

55. RELIGION AND CONSCIENCE

RELIGION IS NOT SOMETHING that you and I can dictate. Religion is the worship of God, and therefore it is a matter of conscience. Each of us must decide how we are going to worship.

> *O come, let us worship and bow down,*
> *let us kneel before the LORD, our Maker!*

— PSALM 95:6

56. FOCUSED LIVES

LET'S NOT LIVE DISTRACTED lives.

But the Lord answered her, "Martha, Martha, you are worried and distracted by many things; there is need of only one thing. Mary has chosen the better part, which will not be taken away from her."

— LUKE 10:41-42

57. THE GIFT OF GIVING

YOU NEED TO LEARN how to give, not to give because you have to give, but because you want to give.

"Give, and it will be given to you. A good measure, pressed down, shaken together, running over, will be put into your lap; for the measure you give will be the measure you get back."

— LUKE 6:38

58. THE DUTY OF PRIESTS

BE HOLY AND TEACH us to become holy also. Teach us prayers that will purify our hearts and help us grow in our faith. Remind us of the importance of meditation on Jesus, our source of love and service.

It is even more obvious when another priest arises, resembling Melchizedek one who has become a priest, not through a legal requirement concerning physical descent, but through the power of an indestructible life. For it is attested of him,

"You are a priest forever,
according to the order of Melchizedek."

— HEBREWS 7:15-17

59. THE HEM OF HIS GARMENT

LOVE HAS A HEM to her garment that reaches to the very dust.

Now there was a woman who had been suffering from hemorrhages for twelve years; and though she had spent all she had on physicians, no one could cure her. She came up behind him and touched the fringe of his clothes, and immediately her hemorrhage stopped. Then Jesus asked, 'Who touched me?' When all denied it, Peter said, "Master, the crowds surround you and press in on you." But Jesus said, "Someone touched me; for I noticed that power had gone out from me." When the woman saw that she could not remain hidden, she came trembling; and falling down before him, she declared in the presence of all the people why she had touched him, and how she had been immediately healed.

— LUKE 8:43–47

60. LOVING ONE ANOTHER

JESUS DID NOT SAY, "Love the whole world." He said, "Love one another."

"This is my commandment, that you love one another as I have loved you. No one has greater love than this, to lay down one's life for one's friends."

— JOHN 15:12-13

61. Bloom Where You Are Planted

It does not matter who we are, it does not matter what our profession is, in other words, what we do. It does not matter what our nationality is, or whether we are rich or poor. Whatever our state in life, above all we are children of God, the work of his hands.

Were you a slave when called? Do not be concerned about it. Even if you can gain your freedom, make use of your present condition now more than ever.

— 1 Corinthians 7:21

62. Love to Win the World

PRAY THAT YOU AND I don't employ bombs and cannons to conquer the world. Let us use love and compassion to win the world.

I will make for you a covenant on that day with the wild animals, the birds of the air, and the creeping things of the ground; and I will abolish the bow, the sword, and war from the land; and I will make you lie down in safety.

— HOSEA 2:18

63. It Was Good

How can we complain against God for the poverty and suffering that exist in the world? Can we honestly do so? God saw that everything was good. What we do with things is another matter.

God saw everything that he had made, and indeed, it was very good.
— Genesis 1:31

64. THE FREEDOM OF POVERTY

WHAT IS POVERTY? . . . It is a freedom so that what I possess doesn't own me, so that what I possess doesn't hold me down, so that my possessions don't keep me from sharing or giving of myself.

Jesus said to him, "If you wish to be perfect, go, sell your possessions, and give the money to the poor, and you will have treasure in heaven; then come, follow me."

— MATTHEW 19:21

65. LET GOD BE GOD

GOD HAS HIS OWN ways of working in the hearts of men and we do not know how close he is to each one. We have no right to condemn, to judge, or to say things that can hurt other people for their beliefs.

For my thoughts are not your thoughts, nor are your ways my ways, says the Lord.

— ISAIAH 55:8

66. MEASURE OF LOVE

THE IMPORTANT THING IS not how much we accomplish, but how much love we put into our deeds every day. That is the measure of our love for God.

My child, perform your tasks with humility;
then you will be loved by those whom God accepts.
— ECCLESIASTICUS 3:17

67. Open Your Hand

IF OUR POOR HAVE at times starved to death, it is not because God doesn't care for them. Rather it is because you and I have refused to give food to them.

Since there will never cease to be some in need on the earth, I therefore command you, "Open your hand to the poor and needy neighbor in your land."

— Deuteronomy 15:11

68. A STILL, SMALL VOICE

WE NEED TO FIND God and he cannot be found in noise and restlessness.

Now there was a great wind, so strong that it was splitting mountains and breaking rocks in pieces before the LORD, but the LORD was not in the wind; and after the wind an earthquake, but the LORD was not in the earthquake; and after the earthquake a fire, but the LORD was not in the fire; and after the fire a sound of sheer silence. When Elijah heard it, he wrapped his face in his mantle and went out and stood at the entrance of the cave. Then there came a voice to him that said, "What are you doing here, Elijah?"

— 1 KINGS 19:11-13

69. WORK FOR THE LORD

NEVER DO THE WORK carelessly because you wish to hide your gifts. . . . The talents God has given you are not yours — they have been given to you for your use, for the glory of God.

Whatever your task, put yourselves into it, as done for the Lord and not for your masters.

— COLOSSIANS 3:23

70. TO SUFFER WITH CHRIST

SUFFERING IN AND OF itself is useless, but suffering which is a share in the passion of Christ is a marvelous gift for human life.

Beloved, do not be surprised at the fiery ordeal that is taking place among you to test you, as though something strange were happening to you. But rejoice insofar as you are sharing Christ's sufferings, so that you may also be glad and shout for joy when his glory is revealed.

— I PETER 4:12–13

71. SPREADING THE GOSPEL

WE HAVE TO CARRY our Lord to places where he has not walked before.

And he said to them, "Go into all the world and proclaim the good news to the whole creation."

— MARK 16:15

72. Loving the Lord

You must love with your time, your hands, and your hearts. You need to share all that you have.

He said to him, "'You shall love the Lord your God with all your heart, and with all your soul, and with all your mind.' This is the greatest and first commandment."

— Matthew 22:37-38

73. THE BALM OF KINDNESS

KINDNESS HAS CONVERTED MORE people than zeal, science, or eloquence.

As God's chosen ones, holy and beloved, clothe yourselves with compassion, kindness, humility, meekness, and patience.

— COLOSSIANS 3:12

74. Drop in the Ocean

All that work is only a drop in the ocean, but if we neglect to put in that drop, the ocean will be less.

He looked up and saw rich people putting their gifts into the treasury; he also saw a poor widow put in two small copper coins. He said, "Truly I tell you, this poor widow has put in more than all of them; for all of them have contributed out of their abundance, but she out of her poverty has put in all she had to live on."

— Luke 21:1-4

75. THE DUTY OF HOLINESS

Holiness is not the luxury of the few. It is a simple duty for each one of us.

Pursue peace with everyone, and the holiness without which no one will see the Lord.

— HEBREWS 12:14

76. REAL LOVE

LOVE, TO BE REAL, must cost; it must hurt; it must empty us of self.

Little children, let us love, not in word or speech, but in truth and action.

— 1 JOHN 3:18

77. THE LIGHT OF THE WORLD

When you look at the inner workings of electrical things, often you see small and big wires, new and old, cheap and expensive lined up. Until the current passes through them there will be no light. That wire is you and me. The current is God. We have the power to let the current pass through us, use us, produce the light of the world — Jesus. Or we can refuse to be used and allow darkness to spread.

Again Jesus spoke to them, saying, "I am the light of the world. Whoever follows me will never walk in darkness but will have the light of life."

— John 8:12

78. Fruitful Branches

IF WE NEGLECT PRAYER and if the branch is not connected with the vine, it will die. That connecting of the branch to the vine is prayer.

"I am the vine, you are the branches. Those who abide in me and I in them bear much fruit, because apart from me you can do nothing."
— JOHN 15:5

79. In the Palm of His Hand

Every time God looks at his hand, he sees me there. He sees you there too.

> *Can a woman forget her nursing-child,*
> *or show no compassion for the child of her womb?*
> *Even these may forget,*
> *yet I will not forget you.*
> *See, I have inscribed you on the palms of my hands;*
> *your walls are continually before me.*

— Isaiah 49:15-16

80. MARY'S SONG

THE *MAGNIFICAT* IS OUR Lady's prayer of thanks. She can help us to love Jesus best; she is the one who can show us the shortest way to Jesus.

And Mary said,
  "My soul magnifies the Lord,
    and my spirit rejoices in God my Savior,
for he has looked with favor on the lowliness of his servant.
    Surely, from now on all generations will call me blessed."

— LUKE 1:46-48

81. LIKE A LITTLE CHILD

How do you pray? You should go to God like a little child. A child has no difficulty expressing his little mind in simple words which say so much.

He called a child, whom he put among them, and said, "Truly I tell you, unless you change and become like children, you will never enter the kingdom of heaven."

— MATTHEW 18:2-3

82. The Poor with You

Before anything else, look for the poor in your own homes and on the street where you live.

"For you always have the poor with you, but you will not always have me."

— Matthew 26:11

83. PRAYING IN THE SPIRIT

Ask the Holy Spirit to pray in you. Learn to pray, love to pray, and pray often. Feel the need to pray and to want to pray.

Likewise the Spirit helps us in our weakness; for we do not know how to pray as we ought, but that very Spirit intercedes with sighs too deep for words. And God, who searches the heart, knows what is the mind of the Spirit, because the Spirit intercedes for the saints according to the will of God.

— ROMANS 8:26-27

84. Content in All Things

It would be a defect to speak about food or to complain about what is served. . . . If dishes taste well, thank God! If not, thank him still, and thank him even more because he has given you an opportunity to imitate our Savior in his poverty.

Not that I am referring to being in need; for I have learned to be content with whatever I have. I know what it is to have little, and I know what it is to have plenty. In any and all circumstances I have learned the secret of being well-fed and of going hungry, of having plenty and of being in need.

— Philippians 4:11-12

85. TAKE UP YOUR CROSS

DIFFICULT, YES. IT'S MEANT to be difficult. . . . We are not the only ones that have to obey. Red light, green light, that's also obedience.

He called the crowd with his disciples, and said to them, "If any want to become my followers, let them deny themselves and take up their cross and follow me."

— MARK 8:34

86. A Second Nazareth

WE MUST MAKE OUR home like a second "Nazareth" where Jesus can come and live with us.

When they had finished everything required by the law of the Lord, they returned to Galilee, to their own town of Nazareth.

— LUKE 2:39

87. GOD'S GOOD NEWS

WHAT IS THE GOOD news? The good news is that God will love the world through each one of you. You are God's good news, you are God's love in action.

"I ask not only on behalf of these, but also on behalf of those who will believe in me through their word, that they may all be one. As you, Father, are in me and I am in you, may they also be in us, so that the world may believe that you have sent me."

— JOHN 17:20-21

88. UNHEALTHY COMPANY

MAYBE [JESUS] WANTS YOU just to smile, to say, "May I," to be on time, or to give up an unhealthy friendship.

Do not be deceived:
"Bad company ruins good morals."

— 1 CORINTHIANS 15:33

89. THE VALUE OF WORK

IF YOUR WORK IS slapdash, then your love for God is slapdash.

Whatever your hand finds to do, do it with all your might; for there is no work or thought or knowledge or wisdom in Sheol, to which you are going.

— ECCLESIASTES 9:10

90. FOR THE LORD

WHEN YOU ARE COOKING, washing clothes, working hard in the office, do it all with joy. That will be your love for God in action!

Whatever your task, put yourselves into it, as done for the Lord and not for your masters.

— COLOSSIANS 3:23

91. SPIRITUAL FEEDING

WE HAVE TO FEED ourselves. We can die from spiritual starvation. We must be filled continually, like a machine. When one little thing in the machine is not working, then the whole machine is not working properly.

For though by this time you ought to be teachers, you need someone to teach you again the basic elements of the oracles of God. You need milk, not solid food; for everyone who lives on milk, being still an infant, is unskilled in the word of righteousness. But solid food is for the mature, for those whose faculties have been trained by practice to distinguish good from evil.

— HEBREWS 5:12-14

92. IF YOU DO NOT HAVE LOVE

YOU MAY BE EXHAUSTED with work — you may even kill yourself — but unless your work is interwoven with love, it is useless.

If I speak in the tongues of mortals and of angels, but do not have love, I am a noisy gong or a clanging cymbal. And if I have prophetic powers, and understand all mysteries and all knowledge, and if I have all faith, so as to remove mountains, but do not have love, I am nothing. If I give away all my possessions, and if I hand over my body so that I may boast, but do not have love, I gain nothing.

— 1 CORINTHIANS 13:1–3

93. CLOTHED IN DIGNITY

NAKEDNESS IS NOT ONLY the need for a piece of clothing. Nakedness is the need for human dignity which people sometimes lose, which we unjustly take away from the poor.

"Lord, when was it that we saw you hungry or thirsty or a stranger or naked or sick or in prison, and did not take care of you?" Then he will answer them, "Truly I tell you, just as you did not do it to one of the least of these, you did not do it to me."

— MATTHEW 25:44-45

94. GOD IS LOVE

IF WE HAVE BEEN created in the image of God, then we have been created to love, because God is love.

Whoever does not love does not know God, for God is love.
— 1 JOHN 4:8

95. ALONE WITH GOD

YOU ARE CALLED TO pray, to be alone with Jesus. I haven't the slightest doubt that if your hearts are clean, you will surely hear the voice of God in your heart.

"But whenever you pray, go into your room and shut the door and pray to your Father who is in secret; and your Father who sees in secret will reward you."

— MATTHEW 6:6

96. THE WAY OF TRUTH

JESUS CANNOT DECEIVE US.

Jesus said to him, "I am the way, and the truth, and the life. No one comes to the Father except through me. If you know me, you will know my Father also. From now on you do know him and have seen him."

— JOHN 14:6-7

97. Sign of Pride

Don't give in to discouragement. . . . If you are discouraged, it is a sign of pride because it shows you trust in your own powers.

When pride comes, then comes disgrace;
but wisdom is with the humble.

— Proverbs 11:2

98. FAITH AND WORKS

FAITH IN ACTION IS service. Faith in action becomes a delight because it gives you the opportunity of putting your love for Christ into action — it is meeting Christ, serving Christ.

What good is it, my brothers and sisters, if you say you have faith but do not have works? Can faith save you? If a brother or sister is naked and lacks daily food, and one of you says to them, "Go in peace; keep warm and eat your fill," and yet you do not supply their bodily needs, what is the good of that? So faith by itself, if it has no works, is dead.

— JAMES 2:14-17

99. Image of a Suffering God

WHEN ALL OF US recognize that our suffering neighbor is the image of God himself and when we understand the consequences of that truth. That day poverty will no longer exist.

It was fitting that God, for whom and through whom all things exist, in bringing many children to glory, should make the pioneer of their salvation perfect through sufferings.

—HEBREWS 2:10

100. THE FUTURE

WE MUST NEVER GET into the habit of being preoccupied with the future. There is no reason to do so. God is there.

"Heaven and earth will pass away, but my words will not pass away."
— MATTHEW 24:35